THE
WOODS
HOLD
US

THE
WOODS
HOLD
US

Poems

MAKANI SPEIER-BRITO

atmosphere press

CONTENTS

~*~

Blood relations are only one aspect of a family, and my poems aim to demonstrate that true families are formed when people stay with one another. My poems explore the instances where families are created and the intricate feelings shown between people who bond to one another. Dialogue intermingles with imagery to capture these instances and feelings. America's culture of speed and efficiency is challenged by my poems which encourage patience. I create breathe in between the words by allowing space to let the reader pause and immerse themselves into the scene of the poem.

There are families formed solely through a sense of duty. People who marry but do not love one another. They are like houses with people living in them but are absent of the warmth that is found in a home. There are dysfunctional families who cut each other with their words. I find that the truest families are those that are formed that create an atmosphere of understanding, peace, acceptance, patience and love.

~*~

Rearview Mirror

I gaze out of the moving window,
Bedan and Alison gaze at me.

I tell them of my parents' divorce
I observe their comfort,
their true love,
their life of goodness,
their life of safety and serenity.

Do they see me as a cracked marble?
His dad glances into the rearview mirror,
his eyes glint to mine.

I feel unusually small,
unusually flawed
unusually judged
I sense their peak of curiosity
my hint of imperfection.

I glance back to the rolling hills.
My love, hold my hand,
don't be so quick to judge me.

Daughter

I knew we would always be here in the last day of
    January.
lifted into trees by a soft hand.
Peer out,
out to the bay peeking through the fog
to the wonder of being
being here not being there.
The past folding and refolding, folding again.

The edges become soft and weary.
Daughters become lovers.

A cabin shakes
his life drifts away into the stormy night
his hands are still wrapped around her body.

The white foam of crashing seas peel back
taking another into its soft waves.
A mother taking back her child.

We used to be young,
we used to think of the horizon as endless,
but into the light you gazed out.

Full Moon

White sand bathes in moon glow,
crystalizing rocks to pearls,
shine cool, shine composed.
Curved bones
jut from the sand,
cliff upon cliff
fade into one another,
looming pale and ebony.

Casey and I drink
the midnight milk
and race with white fluid in our veins.
Pound our feet to sand
and break the animal tracks.

Black shadows cast from driftwood
and the curved tide
endlessly crashing.
Waves pulling and retreating,
infinite silk ribbon,
we stumble upon rib bones.

Mom

Mom slams the car door.
She walks from the car
her car parked under banana trees
her clogs splat on the ground.

She looks like
a wet,
frightened
dog.

She carries a tea mug
hurriedly through the warm rain

"Mahukona?"
she hisses.
A swim
she pleads
after she talks about
traveling with dad.

She knows she has survived.
As she dives into the salt water.

Simple Mattress

My mom's bed
seems smaller—

Was it always this small?
How did the two of us
fit together?
We did.

I grew longer
dozing in her bed
as she read to me,
I rested in the crook of her arm.

Later, we would read side by side
I would fall to sleep first,
she would turn out the light.

Now, I sleep on this
simple mattress: alone
and overgrown.

Chemo

All the hair you lost
is gathered
in God's silky hands.

I stroke
your face
as we levitate
over the scintillating waters
and there
is peace
in that
moment.

I look to my hand
on your wrinkled cheek.
As the white light casts upon your face,
you become the light
while my hand
is tethered to the earth.

Dad

I swallow my words.
Beneath his fingernails
the scent of garlic
lingers plump and proud.

The dogs are fighting,
gnarled faces in the surf;
dad laughs at their sharp barks,
he kicks up the waves.

Limp black hair
salted with
white strands.

Ahead on the white sand,
I watch him stagger.

Mijo

They wait

and lean against the wire fence,

hands burrowed in their thick, camel colored jackets

and heads bowed in black baseball caps.

It's 7am

they are standing on the sidewalk

black mustached

a forlorn look on their faces

They are weary

and I wonder what they have seen.

They murmur *hello*

in a thick accent

they rise early

grip the few crumpled dollars in their pants' pocket.

They wait

for the white man in his big white pick-up truck

to sneak into the parking lot

and motion three fingers in the air

that's how many he needs for the day.

The white man doesn't look in their direction.

It's difficult to say who is the devil here:

the white man needs workers for cheap

he pays for their meals

and they need work

without papers,

they'll suffer anything for a few more dollars.

The devil is the system

It says

You are an alien

repeats

You haven't passed my rules

you are not a citizen

you are less than.

They all wear heavy backpacks

heavy with their past tears

and dirt that just stays on their hands

even after they wash.

They light up a smoke in the early morning,

They face the cement and stare down at their worn, black

    shoes.

silk water

sweet dusk
we walk on a dirt road
wet in summer
damp against my chest
we return from your neighbor's pool

I could live in the silence of our memory
heart husk
you were so bright
I could feel God hugging us

the first blades of our youth
sprout from Mother Earth
I remember feeling silky water
stroke our thighs

Stepmom

She was beautiful
The archetype of male adoration
A blonde model
From NYC socialites
The higher class, the praised people.

The world shaped her to their desires
She was blue-eyed, innocent and sixteen,
They seduced her to the catwalk
Fawned over her beauty: captured it, stole it, critiqued it.
That's all they wanted from her,
That's all they saw.

She drank their praise
Became addicted to youth, to beauty, to the male gaze
Wielded her beauty as a power to survive.

She followed what the world valued:
Money, dresses, material markers of success.

Blindly, she thought that's all she needed.

Injected silicon into her breasts,
Was shaped, perfected,
Isolated.

Years later,
married to a doctor,
Wealthy,
She was never filled up
Never felt complete
But on the outside
All seemed perfect.

The blue in her eye dimmed
Its sparkle dulled
She felt darkness everyday
And every day, no one believed her.

According to her mother, she had succeeded:
Married a doctor, set for life with the latest clothes
Stylish, sophisticated, perfect,
But on the inside,
She was drowning.

Like the world, her husband only valued her as a trophy
To be displayed, polished and boasted to other husbands.

She hid bottles around their spacious home,
She hid her shame,
Tried to feel at ease with every swig.

Until one day, her forgotten friend wanted to meet for

lunch,
A friend from high school, the one she turned her back on
when she pursued modeling.

They sat down at a quiet cafe,
Over delicate plates of food,
She asked quietly, peered deep into her blue eyes:
"How do you feel?"

The stepmom burst in tears.

From that day forward,
She did take the small yet powerful steps towards
      recovery,
Towards the light.

Away from the shallow lies everyone believed about her.

In those salty tears, she was reborn.

Meeting the Parents

Do you remember when you got drunk at my parents'
house during dinner?
while the girl with cancer was chit-chatting
about driving around the U.S. in her trailer
to see all
the national parks before she died.

You played the piano
grinning and swaying.

I loved you then in that
moment and even later
when you slurred,
You raw, exquisite beauty.

Genesis

A pull to the white light
green slips through winter's fingers
genesis.
Your lips echo Persian poems
your last name
a poem in itself.

There is a pull to those April hills.
We'll never understand
the intertwining of God's plan
but we feel a familiar stillness
deep and humming low.

A soft knowing
those that hum at night for hopes across the seas.
To a land free
of an enchanted reality.

As you clasp the bottle
and retell those stories from your time in Germany.
We listen, we listen
and hum to the rhythm of God's plan.

Baba

Salt of the earth
Sturdy as a redwood tree
You now return to the earth
and we pray.

I remember your soft red flannel
your iron resolve
the way you folded your arms
to guard your soft, gentle heart.

Your eyes twinkled when you told me about your football
    days
and the way I see it, you never stopped coaching,
you coached your kids and then your grandkids.
You told me how you were yanked out of college
to fight foreign men on foreign lands.

Sadness lay in your eyes when you shared
these stories.
Joy in your eyes
When you called Nana your bride.
We hope for a lasting love like yours.

Your common sense was a gift,
your love selfless and filled with peace.

May you always feel the peace and security you gave us.
You wished for simple things:
a wife, children and a cabin by the sea. You succeeded.
May the ocean breeze carry you to heaven's gate.
We will always cherish your love.

I See You

I feel the essence of you
Everywhere I go.

In the shade of pine trees
The humid earth
The river smoothly sliding over pebbles.

You are the peace of an August afternoon.
The wisdom of the ancient trees.
The bright youth of a thousand doves taking flight…
white wings that pass and catch the glint of a setting sun.

In awe, I gaze.

You can't be found
Yet every day,
I see you.

Cleanse

Do you know the
salted hair of your dad, the
chirp of your mom, the deep
rootedness, the light streaming
from the lemon slice
window, you know a low
hum...

I surrender to the beauty of those memories.

I surrender to your tender light.

Your father gives water to
the plants, I watch him
water the dry, cracked yellowed
earth and how he prays
and prays for rain.

Hope and pride reflected in
your father's smooth boyish face,

his expectation:

that I may bear him grandchildren.
your fear.

Your desperation to rewind,
to jog backwards in time:
to when grapes were provided on the dining room table,
before you needed to buy your own grapes,
I feel your desperation
and fear to return, your

stubborn refusal to face
me, to see your role, to see
and understand where and how you stand.

Henna

Ruchita carefully pushes the brown ink into my palm.
The design is delicate
her eyes shiny black stones
as she gazes to the wet ink
she blesses me
she marks me
ink of love
ink of commitment
in that airy room
the heat wave blankets the world outside these walls.
Her every movement has meaning
every word she speaks holds truth, traces depth.

Do we jump?

We wake up
another day
me to you
you to me
the mist feels
fine
the fog always clears.

Look,
this too shall pass,
this *too* shall pass.

Our arms create
a chain
of words
create
cool rivers
flowing through
the empty
rock pathways
of our hearts
the cool water
flows between
jagged, black rock.

One day we may wake
and say "enough"
for the river
has dried.

One day the oceans
may rise
we can't control
the future
we can't control
anything.

For now,
You are here
I am here
As we affirm
the uncertainty.

As we affirm
the fear
as we affirm
"I like us"
we look over the edge
the waterfall
at the crashing water
below
the cool cleansing
waters
and the jagged
rocks
that could
          smash
                    our
                         hearts
  if we jump

  do we jump?

Newlywed Dance

In the light
of Chinese lanterns
dust swirls
beneath her
buttermilk dress.

His hands slung low
around her hips;
they swirl.

Bending arms
they are harmony
gray-haired men
sway in the shadows
gaze at the
newly wed dance.

A family

Listen;
when you played the mattress
in blue light
I played the sheet.
I lay
stacked
on your body
belly down.

A tiny line between your legs
your shoulders
a soft, white mound
a little boy
runs
to our room
he wants to be the pillow.

We three are a family.

Tea Cakes

violet leaves
sweet gaze of my honey bee
white linen
sun-soaked stares
these are the moments
of wine in glasses
soft stillness
in small white houses
where the porch holds us.

My toes are warmed by your blanket
all my hands come to your cheek
I hold amber sunshine in your eye,
my late August love.

When the wind is still,
your palms stroke my legs beneath the small table
we take tastes of small pears dipped in warm fondue.

My sweet love, is this what it will be like growing old with
    you?

Ruchita's Curtains

I can feel her hurt,
Ruchita made a home with a man whom she does not love
a still home,
a home where she hangs her paintings.

All the walls are white
all the rooms carry a history.
Though she is aging slowly,
the light in her home is young.

Ruchita wants me to be her daughter-in-law
her son brought me home,
she puts a necklace of white diamonds simply around my
        neck.

She puts more jewels that lay resting on my forehead,
I feel her peace.
I feel her taking me into the nestled home of her family.

The white curtains are long,
they blow gently in the breeze
like a woman's long white skirt.

Tiny Paper Cranes

Do you fold over her like white paper?
Does she dip her hair in paint
reds, blues and the lightest baby pink?

Does she fold beneath you?
Like paper cranes that arch their necks,
do you bend your necks to hold close the warmth and
electric heat?

I wonder.

Where do you both go to escape from the cold?
Does she skip over railroad tracks?
Do you hold her hand?
Do you gently rub your thumb over her fingers
and whisper *my love*
?

Kid

The old woman says to me:
You need to be more assertive and more aggressive, kid.
The world is harsh out there.
She feeds the two metal bowls for her blind cats
The cats are her children, meandering around the worn
    carpet
I was like her granddaughter she said matter of factly
resting on the plush pillows
she spoke of the one man she truly loved
like muttering a grocery list
he was an artist, found in his garage one day
eternally asleep, the engine of his car running.
The painting of him
hung in her living room
the paint caked, his frozen eyes to the brink of tears
I listen and nod.
I wonder what happened to her.

One day will I also hang a painting of my love?
Will I care for cats instead of my own kin?
For now,
I find comfort in drifting to sleep with the memory of you
on repeat.

Son

Black hair grows over each knuckle on his dirty fingers,
an overgrowth, a black patch.

Who warms his fingers at night?
He cozies up to a newspaper bed on a slab of cold cement.
He howls to the moon through his watery eyes.

Each nod is a curse,

each *hello*
a plea.

Through the Marshes

we meet part way on the bridge
and even before we meet,
you blow on my dandelion heart
with your sweet breath
and scatter me in the wind.

Your hands dry
but that sacred center in your green eye
I could swim in forever
through the rested marshes where we will meet
when the cattails bend their heads
where you will gently reach for my naked body
and in the river we will swim
backwards in time
when society wouldn't pull you away
its wasted plastic bags,
its urgency
concrete,
and all its predators.

Where you would stay and be nourished
where we could nourish each other
in the silent autumn air.

Stuffy Inside

The Air Quality Index for today reads:
'Unhealthy' in red.
The air is as toxic inside as it is outside,
we are stuck.

You fling spiteful words into the air
your words drag heavy over us
and create a heavy smog

As you stress-eat another chocolate muffin,
you say we are waiting
for a tectonic plate to shift,
shake everything to the ground.

Stay indoors the news reports say,
but only forgiveness will clear the air between us.
For now, I will wear a white mask
put it over my face to protect myself from you.
Until the air clears,
I will wait.

Your words are toxic particles:
I will not inhale them.

Lost and Found

Your words
Your glance
Judge and criticize.

My words sprout out
New and lovely,
You try to mow them down.

Every glance, you stare, aware
And hold your head up a bit higher.

Why are you still so afraid?
Afraid of my words, so piercing, so clear?

Aware of my unencumbered tongue, loose and wild?

I'm giddy with the word.

This childish glint in my eye, you can not dull.
There is God protecting me always
And when you try to sting me,
You are flicked off like a bug on the windshield.

I feel sorry for you,
For you, have lost the bounce and zeal of creativity.

For you, have been dulled and subdued.

You feel like something is missing, but what?

You can't quite put your finger on it.
You have lost your soul.
May you find it soon.

Imprint

delicate breeze

              I see the ocean

churning cold blue

when the world gets soggy

              to the sand I go

to meditate with the waves

and release your lies

              from my chest

Bath to Bed

Clouded,
warm
milky water
eucalyptus.

The cement
floor is
wet.

I grip my
hands to
the porcelain tub.

Satin water
slips
from my neck.

Outside
shriveled green limes
dangle from branches.

I hear
clucking,
thumping of a basketball.
Abuelita speaking

Her voice
Like scolding:
"Ella quiere descansar para un año."
"Puedes hacer eso en los Estado Unidos."

Sliding into sheets,
her voice dims.

Laying Luna
lifts her
eyes
between
my thumbs.

Love is to Lessen the Suffering

I step lightly

I step with care

you protect
me

your hand cuddled
close

I am in your cocoon
in a shell
of warmth and pure light.

The Woods Hold Us

I am full.
Your interlaced
pink hands
soft palms
I am a pillow.

Your head rests deep peace,
deep slumber,
sweet cusp of dreams.
You say,
I had a strange dream.
I hold you
easy
without fear
I hold you
as if I have
known you
for lifetimes.

There is one star bright against the pink-drenched sky.

The frozen, sacred dark earth
beneath our steps:
Our fingers interlaced,
Our souls meet again.

The woods hold us
The ancient trees stand as pillars
as you pull my head into your shoulder.

42

ABOUT ATMOSPHERE PRESS

Atmosphere Press is an independent, full-service publisher for excellent books in all genres and for all audiences. Learn more about what we do at atmospherepress.com.

We encourage you to check out some of Atmosphere's latest poetry releases, which are available at Amazon.com and via order from your local bookstore:

The Stargazers, poetry by James McKee
The Pretend Life, poetry by Michelle Brooks
Minnesota and Other Poems, poetry by Daniel N. Nelson
Interviews from the Last Days, sci-fi poetry by Christina Loraine
the oneness of Reality, poetry by Brock Mehler
Drop Dead Red, poetry by Elizabeth Carmer
Aging Without Grace, poetry by Sandra Fox Murphy
No Home Like a Raft, poetry by Martin Jon Porter
Mere Being, poetry by Barry D. Amis
They are Almost Invisible, poetry by Elizabeth Carmer
Auroras over Acadia, poetry by Paul Liebow
Transcendence, poetry and images by Vincent Bahar Towliat
Adrift, poetry by Kristy Peloquin

ABOUT THE AUTHOR

Makani is a graduate of the University of California – Santa Cruz. She received her BA in Literature with a concentration in Creative Writing. Her work has appeared in several publications, including Z Publishing's *Best Emerging Poets of California, CIRQUE, Matchbox Magazine, Red Wheelbarrow, Chinquapin* and *Forever Spoken*. She loves writing about anything that is real and honest. When she's not writing, you can find her singing away, advocating for the zero-waste movement, or wandering around at various farmers markets or at the beach. *The Woods Hold Us* is her first published book. She has pledged to donate 10% of the proceeds from the book to environmental non-profits.